OWEN DAVEY

MAD ABOUT
MONKEYS

FLYING EYE BOOKS

CONTENTS

WHAT ARE MONKEYS?

Monkeys belong to a group of mammals known as primates. Humans are also primates but humans are not monkeys. However, monkeys and humans aren't all that different.

Monkeys evolved around 35 million years ago. Today, they are easily identifiable by their long arms and bodies covered in thick fur and their more exposed faces.

Common Squirrel Monkey

These hands were made for walkin'

Monkeys walk on all fours the majority of the time. Animals that do this are called quadrupeds. Monkeys are able to stand and walk around on their back two legs, but only for a short time.

Home Sweet Home

The type of place where an animal lives is known as their habitat. Some monkeys have a habitat high up in cooler mountainous regions, but most live in warm lowlands like savannahs, plains and more often than not, within tropical rainforests. Many monkeys live in trees to protect themselves from predators. Animals that live in trees are described as being **arboreal**.

Nom Nom

Monkey diets vary from
species to species,
but they can include fruit,
seeds, nuts, leaves, flowers,
insects, spiders, eggs and
even some small animals
like crabs and lizards.

The varied diet
of monkeys

So now you know the basics, let's swing right into an unforgettable adventure across
continents, from the jungles of South America to the highlands of East Africa.
Like us every monkey has its own character and story to tell. So get set to meet
our quirky cousins, and go *Mad about Monkeys!*

IS A MONKEY MY UNCLE?

Many people believe that humans come from monkeys, but this is not true. Humans and monkeys are part of a wider group of mammals called *Primates*.

Monkeys and humans are believed to have shared a common ancestor around 25 to 30 million years ago. Both monkeys and humans evolved from this animal in a variety of different ways until we became the species we are today.

Evolution is the theory of how animals have changed over time. Certain characteristics are passed down from generation to generation to help them survive.

Common Woolly Monkey

Having a longer tail might help a monkey balance better in a tree and make it easier to reach fruit or keep safe from predators. A monkey with a long tail is then more likely to survive to have a baby with a long tail.

The traits of the most successful monkeys, such as a long tail, will thrive in a group and be passed down. Eventually the whole species will have long tails.

The family tree below shows the evolution of primates over the last 45 million years.

Looking at the table, you can see that animals like chimpanzees, gibbons, or lemurs are NOT monkeys. They are all primates but, like humans, have a different classification to monkeys.

The chart also shows that monkeys fall into two distinct groups.

These are called *Old World* monkeys and *New World* monkeys.

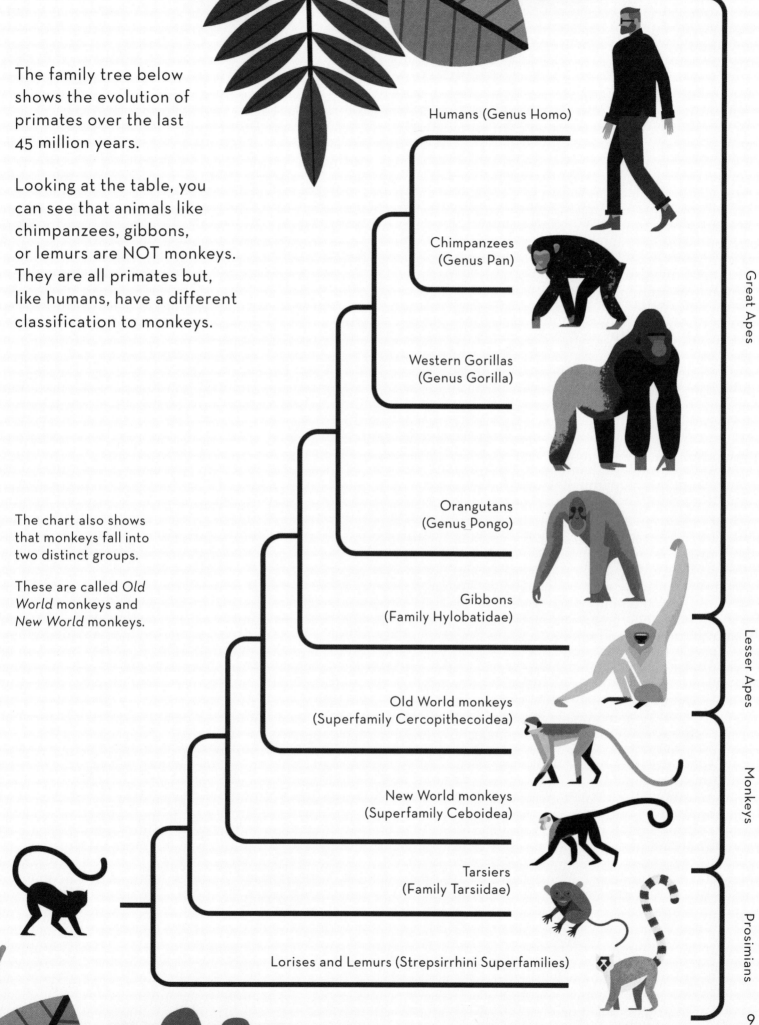

Humans (Genus Homo)

Chimpanzees (Genus Pan)

Western Gorillas (Genus Gorilla)

Orangutans (Genus Pongo)

Gibbons (Family Hylobatidae)

Old World monkeys (Superfamily Cercopithecoidea)

New World monkeys (Superfamily Ceboidea)

Tarsiers (Family Tarsiidae)

Lorises and Lemurs (Strepsirrhini Superfamilies)

Great Apes

Lesser Apes

Monkeys

Prosimians

OLD VS NEW

Monkeys are thought to have evolved in Africa and spread to Asia and then to the Americas. Those that remained in Africa and Asia are *Old World* monkeys and those that evolved in North and South America are *New World* monkeys.

Today, it is possible to tell whether a monkey is classed as *Old World* or *New World* just by looking at it. This page will get you clued up on how to tell the difference!

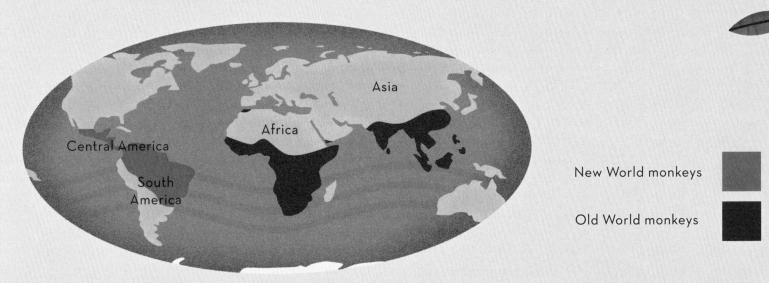

New World monkeys

Old World monkeys

On the Nose

Old World monkeys tend to have narrow noses that point downwards. They have nostrils that are close together and open downwards too. *New World* monkeys, however, have flatter noses and their nostrils are far apart and open sideways.

Celebes Crested Macaque (Old World)
Narrow nose, points downwards

Red Titi (New World)
Flat nose, opens sideways

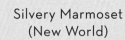
Silvery Marmoset
(New World)

Tree's a Crowd

New World monkeys only ever live in trees, and are small to avoid breaking the branches. Most *Old World* monkeys don't hang around in the trees and can grow much bigger.

Peruvian Black
Spider Monkey
(New World)

The Tail End

Monkeys use their tails to help them with climbing and balancing in the trees, but only *New World* monkeys have something known as a **prehensile tail**. Prehensile means '*able to grasp*'. A prehensile tail is a tail that can act like an extra limb for the monkey.

Take a Seat

Drill
(Old World)

Many species of *Old World* monkeys have strange sitting pads on their bottoms called **ischial callosities**. These hairless pads keep the monkeys more comfortable when they sit down on rocks or trees for long periods of time.

Grivet
(Old World)

Bearded Saki
(New World)

MEET THE GANG!

It's time to don your detective caps! Using everything you've learnt from the previous page, see if you can look at these monkeys and tell whether they are *New World* or *Old World* monkeys.

(If you get stuck, the answers are sideways on the next page.)

A.

Guianan Red Howler monkeys use their strong prehensile tails to hang from trees and pick leaves, fruit, nuts and flowers.

B.

Guereza live in many different types of forests and are found throughout much of Central Africa.

C.
The *Owl-Faced Guenon* has a white stripe on its long nose.

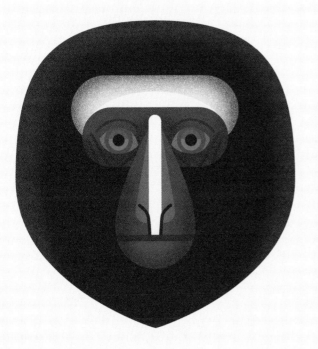

D.
Golden Lion Tamarins move around branches high on the rainforest canopy on all fours. They are closely related to the *Silvery Marmoset*.

E.
This is a *François Langur*. Look at his strange padded bottom!

F.
This *Red-Bellied Titi* is a different species to the *Red Titi* featured on the previous page.

LITTLE AND LARGE

Featured Creatures:
Pygmy Marmoset, New World Monkey, South America

Pygmy Marmosets are the smallest species of monkeys. With a body measuring as little as 12 cm (5 inches) and a tail length of around 17 cm (7 inches).

Harpy Eagle
(a natural predator of
the *Pygmy Marmoset*)

They are the size of a hamster, weigh the same as a pack of cards and can fit in the palm of a human hand. Despite their size, these adorable arboreal primates can leap up to 5 m!

Their small size and sharp claws allow them to move along the smallest branches of trees quickly. They can also turn their heads 180 degrees, when looking for any birds of prey that might be lurking above them.

Pygmy Marmosets have cleverly worked out how to farm sap, a delicious syrup found in trees. They bite off small areas of bark on the tree, then wait a few days. When they return, the sap has collected in the areas they have bitten and the *Pygmy Marmosets* drink their reward. The sap also attracts insects that the marmosets are more than happy to catch and eat as well.

This is a life-size illustration of a Pygmy Marmoset.

Featured Creatures:
Mandrill, Old World Monkey, West Africa

The largest monkey on the planet is the male *Mandrill*. They can reach lengths of approximately 3 ft and weigh over 30 kg. If that isn't scary enough, these monkeys have fangs longer than those of lions!

They are shy creatures though and spend their days on the ground hunting for fruit, seeds, nuts and the occasional small antelope to eat. At night they take to the trees to sleep and protect themselves from prowling predators such as snakes, eagles and leopards.

Red and blue coloured noses and multi-coloured bottoms make mandrills one of the most attractive and beautiful primates.

This is a life-size illustration of a yawning *Mandrill*.

'*But why such colourful bums?*' I hear you ask. Scientists believe that these magnificent rumps are simply used as beacons in the leafy gloom of the forests. When following each other through the forest, the bright rear ends are easy to spot and follow.

15

SOCIAL LIFE

Monkeys are a very social bunch and like to communicate and be with each other, just like we do!

Being in a large community can help protect them from predators, or guard food sources against other animals. It can also help with raising their children.

This is a troop of Hanuman Langurs (Old World)

Monkeys use a variety of noises including chattering, clicking and yelling to communicate. These noises can help them to bond with each other, and alert their friends about potential threats or to warn rival monkeys off their turf.

Diana Monkey
(Old World)

Diana monkeys combine different call sounds to send sentence-like messages through the dense forests to one another. They have unique calls to describe different approaching predators, and even indicate how immediate the threat is. What's even more impressive is that these chatty monkeys can understand the calls of other species of monkey too; you could say that they understand different monkey languages!

Monkeys like to use body language and touch. They sit next to each other to socialise, hold hands and even snuggle together.

One way that monkeys bond is through social grooming. Monkeys sit next to one another and carefully rifle through each other's fur, picking out any dirt or bugs they find hiding. This helps to build bonds and trust with new friends.

KING OF THE SWINGERS

Monkeys usually have a hierarchy within their troops, which means that some monkeys have a higher social status than others. It's like having a medieval king, then lords, knights, and finally peasants. Each monkey has a specific role to play in the group and each role has its own privileges.

Not all interactions between monkeys are friendly. Sometimes they will scrap with each other to gain a better status. This fighting can range from yawns and grinning (often signs of aggression in the monkey world), to full on brawls.

Two fighting
Olive Baboons
(Old World)

Like in many monkey battles, *Baboons* will chase each other, snarling and screaming in an attempt to intimidate their opponent. They are not afraid to punch and bite each other either, and some even attempt to throw their adversaries out of the trees.

If males feel like they have what it takes, they will sometimes challenge the leader monkey to see if they can take control. That means monkey troops often change who is in charge. Studies have shown that when food sources are low, or a group is struggling to find shelter, monkeys will be more likely to fight.

THE GRASS IS ALWAYS GREENER

Featured Creatures:
Gelada, Old World Monkey, Ethiopia, Africa

Geladas are a very special kind of monkey that have a complex society numbering many individuals. Living high up in the mountain meadows of Ethiopia, geladas feed entirely on a diet of grass and other plants.

As the earth's temperature has increased, grass is harder to come by, and they have had to move higher and higher into the chilly mountains to find food.

Because of this, geladas have a thick fur that covers their bodies to keep them warm and the males have an extra long mane of hair over their shoulders known as a cape.

Predators in these mountainous regions include dogs, hyenas, jackals and leopards. At night, geladas clamber over the cliff edges to sleep huddled together on the faces of cliffs. Snoozing on these steep rocky ledges makes it harder for the predators to reach them.

20

Spotted Hyena

African Wild Dog

Ethiopian Wolf

Leopard

There are often disputes about who is in charge and this can be decided by the heart-shaped patch of skin on a gelada's chest. The better his fitness and strength, the brighter a male gelada's chest will become.

On a female gelada, the brightness of this area of skin, coupled with white bumps surrounding it, communicates when she is ready to have babies.

If a score isn't settled by their immediate appearance, the males will pop their lips back over their snout and yawn. By doing this, it exposes their massive teeth and everybody does a quick measure of who has the biggest fangs.

Here is a male *gelada* popping its upper lip over his snout to show everybody who is boss.

I wouldn't mess with him ... **would you?!**

AND THE AWARD GOES TO...

Monkeys are pretty incredible creatures, but some are more incredible than others!

The male howler monkey has a louder call than any other primate and is one of the loudest animals in the world.

Its '*howl*' can be heard from up to three miles away every morning and evening.

He creates this booming growl using a throat pouch that helps the noise resonate. The noise is used to warn off other **Howler monkeys** in the area and protect his patch of the forest.

The prize for fastest monkey in the forest falls to the **Patas monkey**. These moustache-faced primates have been known to reach speeds of 34 mph (55 km/h) when trying to escape predators. These guys are very wary of humans, and usually bolt at the sight of us.

The longest tail of all the primates is that of the female **Spider monkey**. Their tails can reach 3 ft in length, despite the monkey's bodies not even reaching 2 ft long. These incredible tails can carry the spider monkey's entire body weight and even pick up objects as small as a peanut.

Believe it or not, the accolade for being the first primate to fly in space goes to a **Rhesus Macaque** named Albert. On June 14, 1949, Albert II was sent into space by humans to test the effects of space travel on a body.

Despite surviving the flight, he tragically died when the rocket parachute failed. Sadly, many monkeys died during early experiments into space exploration.

The award for best facial hair falls to the **Bearded Emperor Tamarin**. Many monkeys have pretty odd facial hair, but none quite as creative as these guys. The white hair that sits above their upper lip is not only long, but also surprisingly neat and well groomed.

What's more, it's not just the boys that have them; ladies and even their babies have this impressive facial hairstyling too!

WEIRD AND WONDERFUL

Over 260 known species of monkey currently live on our planet and some of them are pretty weird looking. Here are some of the strangest of the bunch!

Night Monkey

The only nocturnal monkey, which means they usually sleep in the day and are up and about at night. Their huge orb-like eyes are great for seeing in the dark.

De Brazza's Monkey

With their long white beard these monkeys were a strong contender for the award of best facial hair.

Red-Shanked Douc Langur

These little guys look like they're wearing make-up. Their colourful appearance and strange faces have led to the inaccurate nickname of the 'Costumed Ape'.

Hamadryas Baboon

Ancient Egyptians considered them to be sacred. One of their gods, Thoth, was regularly drawn as a man with the head of this baboon.

Uakari

Despite their bodies being covered in long hair, their heads are entirely bald and shine a bright pink colour.

White-Faced Saki

These strange looking creatures stay together for life when they are paired.

Proboscis Monkey

Yes, that is his nose! The male proboscis' nose is so long that it dangles down over his mouth. The older they get, the larger the nose becomes.

Golden Snub-Nosed Monkey

These fantastical *Old World* monkeys have long golden fur and beautiful, pale blue faces.

SMARTER THAN THE AVERAGE

What makes monkeys so intelligent and successful as a species is their ability to learn from each other. When a monkey discovers something new, the other monkeys in the troop will copy their behaviour and learn things for themselves.

Some monkeys have learned how to administer medicine. White-faced capuchin monkeys rub their fur with *Giant African Millipedes* and leaves as a form of insect repellent.

Crab-eating macaques spend their days in flooded forests and are unique in the monkey world for swimming underwater. By doing so, they can collect the tasty crabs scuttling along the bottom of the seabed.

This source of food has meant they have developed an amphibious lifestyle, meaning they live on both land and in water. They spend much of their time feeding, socialising, playing and swimming in the flooded areas.

Orange
Mud Crab

Certain monkeys have amazingly worked out how to use tools too. They can also use the same tool in numerous ways: rocks can be used to smash open the shells of nuts or can be bashed together to warn other monkeys of nearby predators.

A Black-Capped Capuchin (Old World) using a rock to smash open a nut.

Crab-eating macaques, also known as Long-tailed macaques (Old World) swim underwater to find crabs to eat.

TOP OF THE CLASS

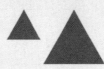

Featured Creatures: Japanese Macaques, Old World monkey, Japan

Japanese macaques are one of the most intelligent monkeys and have displayed some of the most fascinating behaviour in recent studies. Native to the islands of Japan, these macaques are the most northerly-living primates other than humans, and live in a variety of climates ranging from sub-tropical to sub-arctic forests. Their fur adapts in thickness to allow them to endure the cold snow and ice.

In 1963, a young female Japanese macaque named Mukubili ventured into a natural thermal spa to collect some soybeans. She enjoyed the warm water so much, she stayed for a while. Before long, others from the troop began copying her, and soon, the entire troop began spending time in the hot springs.

Yes, these monkeys relax in warm natural baths! The troop's enjoyment of the warm water became so strong that they began invading human spas, and were eventually given their own area to hang out in.

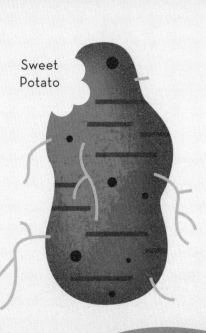

Sweet Potato

Another troop of Japanese macaques washes sweet potatoes in rivers to remove dirt and season their food to make it taste better. The monkeys bite the sweet potato and place it in the sea before eating it. The salt from the seawater acts just like it does when you put salt on your food!

These young snow monkeys have found a unique way of playing. They make snowballs and push them about, throwing or rolling them down hills. Other than it being a lot of fun, this has no purpose whatsoever!

Japanese macaques are a protected species, but the destruction of their habitat has led them to search further afield for food. Sadly, thousands of macaques are killed every year, because they raid the crops of farmers. The macaques have also been known to invade villages and snatch food from people. One macaque is even thought to have lived in Tokyo for several months.

Some cowardly
Black-Capped Capuchins
(New World)

THIEF! HE STOLE MY HANDBAG!

Have you ever wondered why monkeys have such a reputation for being mischievous?
Well, quite frankly, it is a title well deserved...

Monkeys lie to each other. When searching for food, monkeys often travel in groups with
a leader at the front. If this leader has a dishonest streak and discovers a delicious treat,
sometimes they will tell their fellow monkeys that they've seen a predator. All of the other
monkeys will scatter to safety whilst the leader casually gobbles the treat alone.
Sneaky little devils!

Did you know?

Monkey vandalism is common
when people safari through
monkey-inhabited areas. People
often lose luggage, windscreen
wipers and even car bumpers
in these attacks.

A lying little devil eating a banana. Also known as a Black-Capped Capuchin (New World)

Monkeys regularly steal from humans. Businesses and homes can be ransacked in a matter of minutes by these criminal critters. Bolivian Squirrel Monkeys in captivity at London Zoo went through a phase of stealing the sunglasses right off the faces of visitors! Apparently the young ones especially enjoyed looking at themselves in the reflection of the lenses.

Young (and surprisingly fashion conscious) Bolivian Squirrel Monkeys (New World).

MONKEY MYTHOLOGY

Monkeys often appear in folklore, mythology, and religious tales from across the globe.

Spectacled Langur (Old World) representing, Mizaru, Kikazaru and Iwazaru.

'See no evil, hear no evil, speak no evil', is a proverb often represented by three wise monkeys, each displaying different aspects of the saying. The proverb has different meanings around the world, but many people use it in reference to ignoring evil around you.

In the Hindu religion, *Hanuman* is a human-like monkey god who was commander of a monkey army. He had the magical powers of flying or enlarging himself to any size. *Hanuman* is also celebrated for his dedicated service to the God, Lord Rama.

Hanuman

Some people believe that Sun Wukong was the Chinese incarnation of *Hanuman*.

Sun Wukong (also known as the 'Monkey King') is the hero of the classic Chinese novel 'Journey to the West'. He began life as a stone but developed magical powers, and became the leader of a troop of monkeys. He was very mischievous and more than a bit full of himself.

The monkey is a part of the Chinese Zodiac, a calendar system for counting years.

A different animal is assigned to each of the 12 years including Rat, Ox, Tiger, Rabbit, Dragon, Snake, Horse, Sheep, Monkey, Rooster, Dog and Pig.

Monkey is the 9th animal in the zodiac. People born in a year of the monkey are suppose intelligent, lively and creative, but might also be selfish and impatient.

What is your animal year?

DEFORESTATION

It's not an easy time for a lot of monkeys right now. One of the largest threats to monkey populations is the loss of their habitats. Every year, an area of rainforest larger than Wales (or New Jersey) is cut down or destroyed by humans. With less and less space, monkeys struggle to find places to live, eat and play.

As well as being awesome, monkeys play an important part in the ecosystems they live in. Seeds from plants are transported in their poo and deposited around the forest. This helps forests to grow and flourish. Trees produce a lot of oxygen, the gas that we humans need to be able to breathe.

is book is printed
n paper from
ble forests and
ero impact
bitats of
eys.

dly

33

Cotton-Top Tamarin (New World)
Considered Critically Endangered.
Numbers have decreased by over
80% in less than 20 years due
to habitat loss.

Here are some of the ways we affect our global forests and the monkeys that live in them...

A. We create roads to provide better access through the jungle but these only make the rest of the problems worse.

B. Trees are cut down as timber and used to make paper, furniture, and flooring, or burnt for fuel and heating.

C. From poor logging practices, forests have become more at risk from fires, which destroy vast areas.

D. Areas of forest are cleared to make room for crops like oil palm, used in many food and beauty products.

E. Large areas of trees are cleared to create ranchland for cattle to live on.

F. Dams are used to create hydroelectric power but building them can flood large areas of forest.

G. Some areas are cleared for mining purposes in an effort to find precious metals within the earth.

H. There are now over 7 BILLION people on our planet and this number is expected to reach around 10 billion by the end of the century. Many forest areas have fallen victim to cities for our ever-growing species.

What can we do?

Using materials from a rainforest doesn't have to be bad. With careful management of which trees are cut down and by putting restrictions on areas where humans can build, the remaining forests can be protected and some areas will even regenerate. Encourage sustainable forest management by looking for the FSC® label and Rainforest Alliance Certified™ seal when you shop. The little green frog seal is your assurance that a product has been grown and harvested using environmentally and socially responsible practices.

MIX
Paper from
responsible sources
FSC® C101807

INDEX

New World Monkeys

Family Atelidae

Black Howler Monkey (Alouatta caraya) – South America, 22
Brown Spider Monkey (Ateles hybridus) – South America, 23
Common Woolly Monkey (Lagothrix lagotricha) – South America, 8
Guianan Red Howler Monkey (Alouatta macconnelli) – South America, 12
Peruvian Black Spider Monkey (Ateles chamek) – South America, 11

Old World Monkeys

Subfamily Cercopithecinae

Celebes Crested Macaque (Macaca nigra) – South-East Asia, 10
De Brazza's Monkey (Cercopithecus neglectus) – Central Africa, 24
Diana Monkey (Cercopithecus diana) – Western Africa, 17
Drill (Mandrillus leucophaeus) – Central Africa, 11
Gelada (Theropithecus gelada) – Eastern Africa, 20 – 21
Grivet (Chlorocebus aethiops) – North-East Africa, 11
Hamadryas Baboon (Papio hamadryas) – Eastern Africa and Western Asia, 24
Japanese Macaque (Macaca fuscata) – Eastern Asia, 28 – 29
Long-Tailed Macaque (Macaca fascicularis) – South-East Asia, 27
Mandrill (Mandrillus sphinx) – Central Africa, 15
Olive Baboon (Papio anubis) – Central Africa, 18 – 19
Owl-Faced Guenon (Cercopithecus hamlyni) – Central Africa, 13
Patas Monkey (Erythrocebus patas) – Africa, 22
Rhesus Macaque (Macaca mulatta) – Asia, 23
Vervet (Chlorocebus pygerythrus) – South-East Africa, 9

Subfamily Colobinae

François's Langur (Trachypithecus francoisi) – Eastern Asia, 13
Golden Snub-Nosed Monkey (Rhinopithecus roxellana) – Central Asia, 25
Guereza (Colobus guereza) – Central Africa, 12
Hanuman Langur (Semnopithecus hector) – Southern Asia, 16 – 17
Proboscis Monkey (Nasalis larvatus) – South-East Asia, 25
Red-Shanked Douc Langur (Pygathrix nemaeus) – South-East Asia, 24
Spectacled Langur (Trachypithecus obscurus) – South-East Asia, 32

For Gramps,
who always called me 'Monkey'

A special thanks to Dr Nick Crumpton.

Mad about Monkeys © Flying Eye Books 2015.

This is a first edition published in 2015 by Flying Eye Books,
an imprint of Nobrow Ltd. 62 Great Eastern Street, London, EC2A 3QR.

Text and illustrations © Owen Davey 2015.
Owen Davey has asserted his right under the Copyright, Designs and Patents Act, 1988,
to be identified as the Author and illustrator of this Work.

Published in the US by Nobrow (US) Inc.
Printed in Belgium on FSC assured paper.

ISBN: 978-1-909263-57-4

Order from www.flyingeyebooks.com